IN THE WINDS OF HEAVEN

The author, **David Gerrard** was born in Cheshire in 1938 and brought up in Oxfordshire. He studied at Wadham College, Oxford and then spent many years as a television producer with major broadcasting companies in Britain and North America. He has recently turned to writing full-time from his rural base in the Vale of Belvoir.

Cover artist **Ashley Jackson** was born in Penang in 1940 and didn't set foot in Yorkshire until he was ten years old. There he discovered an instant affinity for the Pennine landscape which has provided an inexhaustible inspiration for his work. As popular in the United States as in Britain, his atmospheric paintings are on permanent display at the Ashley Jackson Galleries in Huddersfield.

by the same author

THE REAL SWALEDALE

NORTH EASTERN STEAM — RAILWAY HERITAGE

WALKS IN TEESSIDE

TOURING & EXPLORING NORTHUMBERLAND

TOURING & EXPLORING DURHAM & DURHAM DALES

THE TEAPOT TRAIL — A TASTE OF YORKSHIRE

IN THE WINDS OF HEAVEN

A portrait of Tan Hill Inn, North Yorkshire
David Gerrard.

There is nothing which has yet been contrived by man, by which so much happiness is produced as by a good tavern or inn.
Dr. Samuel Johnson, March 21st, 1776.

CP Printing & Publishing Ltd.
Darlington

First published in 1991
by CP Printing & Publishing Limited
Kellaw Road, Darlington, Co. Durham DL1 4YA.
Telephone (0325) 382360
This edition published 1991

Phototypeset by CP Offset Limited, Darlington.
Printed in England by CP Offset Limited.

FOREWORD

TAN HILL, HIGH ON THE PENNINE WAY

This isolated inn is an attraction to all atmospheric artists who paint in the great cathedral of the open air.

I always try to capture it in the wind and rain, emphasizing the feeling of man's survival on one of Yorkshire's most remote and desolate locations.

It once was a smugglers route, a resting point, and now it is an oasis, to all who walk the Yorkshire Moor in that area. Legend has it that one of its landladies is buried at the rear of the pub.

This pub should be named, "The Moving Inn", as it has been moved in and out of counties for most of its life. Now I am pleased to say it has come back to Yorkshire, it's original birthplace.

Tan Hill always reminds me of a fishing boat out at sea, bobbing about like a cork, surviving all the elements. It is a different Tan Hill on a sunny, cloudless day, when picnickers and day trippers flock to this historic inn, than on days when I have trudged across the rain and windswept moor, with my socks squelching, dying for a pint.

Tan Hill really should be seen to be appreciated.

Ashley Jackson.

For Gayle.

CHAPTER ONE

GETTING HERE CAN BE A PROBLEM...

I'd tried to get to Tan Hill the week before.

It was early December, and on the main road there was only a light dusting of snow scurrying around the traffic. But, as I turned off and started to climb the moorland track, the snow-fall became heavier. Soon, the view through the windscreen resembled a television screen on the blink.

Then the road began to move of its own accord, waving my car from side to side. Reaching an incline, the car slid gently backwards. Several times.

Once again, Tan Hill was cut off.

A week later, I followed the narrow trail the snow-ploughs had carved out. Now it was a bright, moonlit night, the only sign of life occasional Swaledale sheep nudging aside roadside heaps of snow for fodder.

Tan Hill inn entered the headlights — a wall of snow punctured by warmly-glowing windows. The path to the front door lay between the porch wall to the left and a twelve-foot snowdrift to the right.

I opened the door, confidently expecting the welcome due to the only traveller who had braved such a night to reach the most remote hostelry in England.

The inn was packed. It was, after all, Friday night, the traditional evening for anyone within reach of Tan Hill pub to visit.

I negotiated my way through the wall of Barbour jackets, quilted vests and sturdy boots to the bar.

And then listened to the conversation.

A farmer was buying drinks.

"What do you want, Maggie? Besides a bot-smackin', I mean".

"I'll have a bot-smackin'. And a Guinness."

Comfortably seated beside the fire, another farmer recalls a recent triumph. "I had a few little lambs at the auction last Tuesday. I said I want 22 apiece. Dick said, 'Don't you know there's a recession on?' 'I'm having nothing to do with your recession' I said. 'I want £22 for 'em'. 'Aye, well, I came back to £21.50". Gales of laughter: it has been a good price in a difficult year.

Right — Tan Hill Inn at dusk.

The landlady's Jack Russell claims his place in front of the open fire that is kept perpetually burning, day and night, 365 days a year, 'except when we change the grate.'

A toddler staggers across the stone-flagged floor. "You want to get her some clogs. My lass had feet like that. T'clogs straighten them out."

"I'm not well off like these other farmers. Somebody said 'You've no hair.' I said, no. I've been struggling against the current all my bloody life, haven't I?"

Then there's talk about 50-year-old Daphne somewhere down the dale who leaves the farm-gate open when her husband's away as a signal to her lover.

A burly man in his sixties waves a pint-glass towards the fire. "I'm pixed. It's nearly Christmas, I'm looking for a present, I'm looking for a lass."

"You had your chance with my mother-in-law".

"I did, I did and I would have but she went down south again, didn't she?"

I'd only been at Tan Hill for an hour or so but it was obvious that I'd arrived at a very special kind of pub.

CHAPTER TWO

A LITTLE BIT
OF HISTORY

Landlords at Tan Hill have got used to hearing the same question from visitors: "Why on earth is there a pub here?"

It perches on a hill, 1,732ft. above sea level, glorying in its title of the 'highest pub in England'. It is the only dwelling for miles, surrounded in every direction by forbidding hills and heather-swathed moorland. Its surroundings look their best in late summer when the flowering heather creates a shimmering haze of purple.

For the rest of the year, if it's not blanketed by snow, covered in mist or buffeted by winds you can rest your weight against, it presents a limitless expanse of dull brown vegetation. "Everywhere" wrote one 19th century visitor, "a bronze desolation swept to the encircling horizon."

But a hundred years ago, the patrons at the bar didn't question the need for a pub here. Most of them were workers from the nearby coal-mines: others were drivers whose horse-drawn carts stood in long lines outside the pub waiting to be filled with 'crow coal'.

Left — Tan Hill coal pits. At extreme right is Michael Peacock, owner of this pit, whose formidable wife ran the inn for many years.

As the name suggests, it wasn't very good coal. The seam was only about 4 feet deep and it produced a very dirty, dusty fuel. But, as a writer in the "Dalesman" magazine reported: 'Many a farm wife still prefers the small dusty "outcrop" coal which, when mixed with peat, burns with a heating glow and can be banked up at night and, with a little poking, made bright as ever in the morning.'

Working conditions in the mines were grim for both man and beast.

It was also a lot cheaper than the superior coal from the North Durham pits. By the time that had paid its way through the turnpike toll-gates, its cost was way beyond the budgets of struggling Swaledale farmers.

The mines near Tan Hill were certainly working in the 13th century and probably long before that. In 1296, one mine declared a profit for the year of 12d (5p). Perhaps the owners were familiar with the benefits of 'creative accounting'.

Tan Hill coal also helped fuel the lead-smelting kilns of Arkengarthdale. These furnaces were an environmental disaster. In addition to coal they also used wood, stripping Swaledale of the trees that once flourished in its more sheltered areas.

The last mine at Tan Hill closed in 1929. Local workers had defied the call for a General Strike in 1926, — on their marginal incomes too much was at stake. Then, following the strike, improved, toll-free roads meant the better coal reached the dale at affordable prices. Today, the abandoned shafts simply present a dangerous hazard for walkers who stray off the beaten track.

Right — The Moulds coal level. At busy periods, long lines of farmers' carts waited their turn to be filled at the chute. Most drivers waited in the bar.

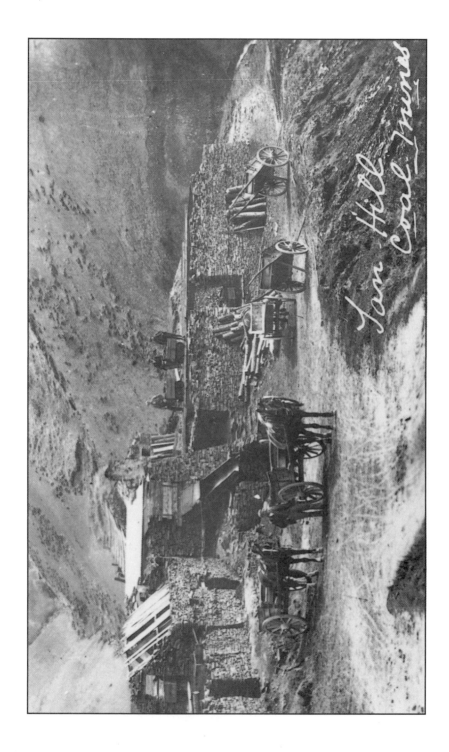

Tom Hill Coal Mines

The first pub at Tan Hill was undoubtedly a very simple hostelry for coal-miners, for pedlars carrying their trinkets between the country fairs of Cumberland and Yorkshire and for Scottish drovers walking their cattle to the rich southern markets.

There's a brief mention in William Camden's guide-book "Britannia", published in 1586: he notes 'a solitary inn' in the middle of a 'mountainous and vast tract'.

The absence of any other records is not surprising since, until recent times, the kind of people who wrote books regarded Upper Swaledale as an area to be avoided, a domain of treacherous weather inhabited only by a few demented peasants.

When William the Conqueror's bureaucrats compiling the Domesday Book for Yorkshire got as far as Reeth in 1085, they looked up the valley and contemptuously wrote it off in one word — "wasteland".

It wasn't until the late 1700s, when the painter J. M. W. Turner made several visits to the region, that its attractions began to be appreciated.

The new railways and roads of the 19th century brought an influx of tourists to Richmond and Reeth, but the rigours of the upper dale around Tan Hill and Keld still discouraged all but the most determined visitors.

When the historian, Robert Clough, stopped off at Tan Hill in 1951, the landlord (Lew Hamilton) described his plans to extend the pub as a tourist centre. 'Nothing came of it' wrote Clough. 'The inn was far too inaccessible in winter.'

Clough was right about the weather, of course: wrong about Tan Hill's potential as a tourist attraction. During the last few years, the pub has become firmly established on the tourist map, a success due in large part to its present owners, Alec and Margaret Baines.

CHAPTER THREE

I'M LOOKING FOR ECCENTRICS...

Auctioneer at Tan Hill Sale,
August 1986.

Alec and Margaret Baines used to live in the bustling Airedale village of Gargrave, 'in a proper cottage with four walls.' Alec had a steady job with the Yorkshire Water Board maintaining reservoirs and also kept a small flock of sheep: Margaret worked part-time as a barmaid at the Mason's Arms.

By chance one evening they caught the end of a television news-item reporting that Tan Hill was up for auction.

"Shall we buy it?" said Margaret jokingly. Alec pondered for a while. "We'll look at it come Sunday."

It was summer, but the inn was smothered in fog.

"What a dump it was. The walls were black with damp, the floors were on a slant. The carpets shone with rat-shit and there was an old settee there. You could hear the mice scurrying around inside it."

"I don't know why, we decided to buy it."

The estate agent told them he had received 500 enquiries about the sale. (He also told them that he would be wearing his pink lame suit at the auction and advised them to wear something that didn't clash.)

Auction day arrived and the Baines levered their way into a bar-room crowded with potential buyers, TV crews and — the largest group — those who were simply curious.

Squeezed into a corner, the auctioneer opened the proceedings: "I'm looking for eccentrics . . ."

The Baines had decided to bid up to £82,000. "I was that nervous," says Margaret, "I had my hand in Alec's trouser-pocket. Then, when the price reached £82,500 and he shouted 'Aye', I thought 'What have we done?' "

The media pounced on Alec. Why had he bought Tan Hill? "Eh, lass, I don't reet know. I've never had a pub before, God knows why I bought it. And," he added straight-faced, "I'm teetotal." The newspapers revelled in it: 'Eccentric Sheep-farmer Buys Highest Pub' one reported.

Another revealed that the new landlord had never pulled a pint in his life.

Somewhat dazed, the Baines drove back to Gargrave. Within minutes there was a phone call offering them £5,000 above their buying price. Later, another caller raised the premium to £10,000. Politely they said 'No': they were now committed to making a going concern of this tiny haven of hospitality in the North Pennines.

It wouldn't be easy. In the previous ten years Tan Hill had seen almost as many landlords. "They'd stay one winter" said a regular "and then they'd be off."

Right — Alec and Margaret Baines behind the bar.
Their busiest day of the year — the Swaledale Sheep Fair — is imminent.

"It struggled a lot o'years, didn't it?" he went on. "Particularly when that Durham lot had it and had a manager in the summer, just a shifty-arsed manager. It'd be 'sell one pint for them and tak' one for hisself.' It'd be making nowt.

Then the bugger set it on fire.

After that it was fettled up again. Someone from Newcastle-side, bloody manager and some sort of a squaw with him. Don't ask him, 'Is that your wife?' — it's his squaw."

The Baines' immediate predecessor as landlord at Tan Hill was Neil Hanson. A crusader for wholesome beer, he had founded the Good Beer Guide and after a year at Tan Hill decided to devote himself full-time to writing about good beer rather than serving it.

Much earlier, between the two World Wars, the inn had been owned by the redoubtable Susan Peacock, a feisty daleswoman who had been born in the pub.

When she herself was about to give birth, she was asked which hospital she would go to. "Nay" she replied, "I was tupped here and I'll be lambed here."

After her death, (also at the pub), there were some half-hearted claims that her ghost haunted the inn in which she had lived for almost half a century. Locals dismissed the stories — it just wasn't the kind of thing the no-nonsense lady would have bothered herself with.

Right — Tan Hill in about 1904.
The neatly dressed children on the left suggest it was a Sunday or holiday.

Alec Baines belongs to the same tradition. When I asked his daughter Kirsty to describe her father, she reflected for a moment and then said "Well, put it this way, he's not a yuppie."

Indeed he is not. Beneath a mop of greying hair, startlingly blue eyes quietly assess those who approach him. If he finds them insincere or pretentious, no comment will be made, but his gaze will stray to more important matters. If you pass this test, you have a friend for life.

Margaret is just as discerning, but much more talkative. She is never happier than when the bar is clamorous with half-a-dozen boisterous conversations — all of which she seems able to keep track of.

Both of them quickly gained the respect of local people.

"The Baines" one of them told me "are doing bloody well, struggling against the National Park and all their fancy damned useless ways but they'll get summat set up. As I look at't, Tan Hill's one of the highlights of National Park. It's highest inn, Pennine Way passes it, everybody stops and has a look, a few chips, this 'n' that, they're good caterers, doing a grand job, unpaid really for what they're doing for the countryside."

CHAPTER FOUR

WE GET
ALL SORTS HERE...

It was midnight when the Baines were aroused by a hammering on the front door. Still drowsy, Margaret opened the door to find two people in full prison garb, complete with black arrows stencilled on their drab grey overalls.

Escaped convicts? Not exactly, just two contestants in a charity 'prison-break' who had to get as far away as possible from South Devon in a twenty-four hour period.

Tan Hill seems to attract unusual visitors.

Britain's most tattooed man turned up one day and caused a sensation. Then there was the man with corks dangling from his hat who claimed he was walking from Land's End to John O'Groats. He was later arrested, having fraudulently extracted a total of £25,000 from trusting people during the course of his walk.

One summer evening, a squad of black-leather-jacketed motor-bikers roaded to a halt outside the pub. Their helmets identified them as 'Satan's Slaves'.

Margaret accosted the burly leader: "Are you going to start any bother?"

"We don't start bother, we finish it."

There was no bother. 'Satan's Slaves' contented themselves with eating dragonflies and when Margaret checked a little later she found them romping with her 4-year-old daughter.

When they left, they departed in strict order of precedence, the President leading his followers down the valley.

Almost as alarming was the arrival of the British Army, just a few days after they had moved in. They awoke to find themselves surrounded by tanks on exercise. "My God" said Alec, "is this how they deliver the meat?"

Right — Farmers would come up the dale selling produce then fill up with Tan Hill coal for the return trip. This photograph is believed to date from the 1890s.

Tan Hill Inn.

Many people first became aware of Tan Hill pub in the mid-1970s when it was featured in a television commercial for Everest double-glazing windows. The popular broadcaster Ted Moult was seen struggling across the moors to the windswept inn, dropping a feather inside the newly-installed windows and then, supping a pint glass of the local brew, delivering the punchline, "This is the only draught you will find up here."

The local council went into special session. The old windows had been replaced without planning permission. They must be removed at once. Their decision was ridiculed in the national newspapers: the double-glazing is still in place.

Some visitors are less welcome than others. Occasionally, the shooting-parties from the Duke of Norfolk's nearby estate drop in and walk out with 'souvenirs' in the form of 'Old Grouse' whiskey ash-trays or water-jugs.

Newspapers, radio and TV are always welcome at Tan Hill: if they can get there. During bad weather, news editors know that the best stories will be found at this isolated inn.

Foreign television stations find Tan Hill just as interesting. A year or so ago, a reporter from Finland's television arrived. In the course of duty he had been sampling British pubs across the country and arrived at Tan Hill in a somewhat enfeebled condition. His comments were very enthusiastic.

A television advertising campaign for double-glazing presented by Ted Moult made Tan Hill nationally famous.

Foreign television stations find Tan Hill just as interesting. A year or so ago, a reporter from Finland's television arrived. In the course of duty he had been sampling British pubs across the country and arrived at Tan Hill in a somewhat enfeebled condition. His comments were very enthusiastic.

"Then there was a group of folk-singers. They arrived with their own piano, wheeled it into the bar, we had a lovely evening, mainly singing."

"And that Robin Hood film, 'Prince of Thieves', they filmed some of that here."

"Japanese, we get a lot of them. We had 20 of them one day. We thought they were going to build a Nissan factory outside."

Pinned to the ceiling-beams in the bar are hundreds of postcards from around the world. "We've been invited to Japan, Australia, America — just about everywhere."

The Baines estimate that about 50,000 people visit Tan Hill each year. Many of them are walkers on the Pennine Way and they deserve a chapter to themselves.

CHAPTER FIVE

IT'S A HARD STEP
TO TAN HILL

The Pennine Way is probably the best-known long-distance path in England. Parts of it can be covered in a gentle afternoon walk: others strain the muscles of the healthiest, most firm-booted walkers as it snakes its way across the backbone of the country.

It starts on a deceptively easy slope leading from the Derbyshire village of Edale and ends, 250 miles later across the Scottish border, at Kirk Yetholm. En route, it takes you through some of the most hostile territory you can find in England: towering peat-hags within which you can lose all sense of direction, falling mists which obscure all the Ordnance Survey maps guidance you were relying on.

You could, of course, be lucky. On clear days, a well-trodden path leads you across wind-scoured hills to the haven of Tan Hill inn. Boots and rucksacks are deposited in the porch, and, clutching a pint of Theakston's Old Peculier Ale, the walkers totter to the nearest settle.

"A lot of Pennine Way walkers don't intend to stay," says Margaret, "but they end up staying. And they come back year after year." Their numbers have increased still more since the opening in 1987 of the Coast to Coast walk from St. Bees in Cumbria to Ravenscar on the Yorkshire coast which crosses the Pennine Way at Keld, a few miles down the dale.

"In t'summer" one regular told me with untypical exaggeration for a Yorkshireman, "t'Pennine Way's black, just black with walkers. And without Tan Hill, it'd be a dismal walk from Swaledale over to Bowes, wouldn't it?"

Most walkers used to either pitch a tent on the moorland around the pub or stay at the Youth Hostel in Keld, but now Tan Hill's new extension offers accommodation for up to 14 people.

When the Baines took over, they produced a Visitors Book especially for the Pennine Way walkers. Much of it is a litany of woe, recording weariness and exasperation: but there are also many expressions of delight at reaching the comfort of Tan Hill. Some of the more printable comments are reproduced here.

EXTRACTS FROM TAN HILL'S VISITORS BOOK FOR PENNINE WAY WALKERS

WHAT ON EARTH DID THEY MEAN?

19. 8.89 Tim — stag night. Good night. Jackie's beautiful girl. Best I've met. Hope to see her next week if she wants to see me.   *(unsigned).*

1. 1.88 I came, I saw, I fell over!   *Mark Robinson, Grimsby.*

30. 7.87 An der Not grisst der Teufel Fliegen, — in England f/grisst er fried breakfast'.

Lars Kramer, West Germany.

A stonebreaker at work near Hoggarth's about 1929. Minor roads around Tan Hill remained primitive until well into the 1930s.

COMPANIONS

11. 4.90 Lisa's started farting like a stag, my dog tries to get sodomized at every opportunity. Am I the only normal person left?　　　　*O. Celt Mackenzie.*

31. 7.90 Never, ever, bring a fashion-conscious, clean-living girl on a walk like the Pennine Way. It'll be sheer hell the whole time and your razor will be bunged up.　　　　*Mark Daniel*
(Answered by Tina Heath): I am not a fashion-conscious, clean-living girl. If I was, I would never have started this walk. Just because I don't fancy living in the same underwear for 2½ weeks — unlike some people I know.

5. 9.89 I've just had three wallies complaining every step of the way. Mike is so fat it was touch and go with many of the squeeze stiles and John's beer-gut completely demolished a wooden stile.
　　　　Pete, Birkenhead.

7. 9.89 I know I should of gone to Tenerife this year where the girls don't wear waterproofs.
(next entry) At least he met some girls!　*(both Anon.)*

9. 8.89 Nick has pissed in his sleeping-bag — just to get a day off.　　　　*(unsigned).*

12ᵖ

Kingsley

KINGSLEY PUBLICATIONS
32 CHATHAM STREET, LEICESTER LE1 6PB

KN 22912

Tan Hill Inn

Somewhere in the middle

of a bog.

KELD

YORKSHIRE

Well, we made it.
After 17 days of rain,
bogs, rain, mist, rain, being
shelled by the army and rain, we
staggered into Yetholm.
Please excuse the wobbly writing — I
am on a bus heading back to
civilisation. It is SUNNY. It is
HOT. I think we are the victims
of some very large side joke.
We love your pub — it's the
best drying room in Britain, and
the bees pretty good too!
Have you ever considered moving it to
Nottingham?

Jim Peacock
Ian Wilson.
Tony Gallagher
Steve Plowright
(we're on the page after number 99)

WHY AM I DOING THIS?

5.10.90 I wonder now why I ever started. There must be some reason but I can't remember what it was.

Brian Reeder, Hemel Hempstead.

31. 7.90 Sodding hot and getting hotter. *Anon.*

18. 8.90 Due to the different types of peat-bog on my trousers, my legs have just been declared a Site of Special Scientific Interest. What can I do? (The rest of the world replies: 'Have a bath'). *M. R. Fuller, Consett.*

9. 9.89 We're having great fun and feeling fine apart from blisters, backache, knee-ache, foot-ache, windchill, frostbite, malnutrition, lack of sleep, lack of beer (and food) but now we've reached here, we'll be alright.

John & Nicky, Preston.

27. 8.89 They tell me there's an end somewhere. *Pete Gilmour.*

27. 8.89 Have got a new ache to go with all the others collected on previous days.

Rick Fulton, Sittinghbourne, Kent.

22. 8.89 Q: What do you call a Pennine Way walker?
A: Anything you like, he won't catch you!!

Andy Seddon.

26. 8.89 My feet feel like someone's grating them with a cheese grater. *Penny.*

13. 8.89 Does it ever stop raining here? *Mary Radley.*

9. 8.89 HYPO—HYDRATION: (vb) i. To be wet. To be incredibly wet. To be so mind-numbingly wet that even your toe-nails start to wrinkle and your nasal hairs become water-logged.
ii. An allergy commonly suffered by long-distance walkers esp. on the Pennine Way. *(Anon.)*

29. 5.87 Where's me legs gone to? *Bryan Forman. S. Wales.*

28. 7.87 Why me? *Corinna Bainbridge.*

1. 8.87 Died 2 days ago. Socks still walking.

David & June Prebble, Spalding.

MEET THE MACHO WALKER

21. 8.89 We're doing it N. to S. not like all the wimps doing it with a carrier bag S. to N.

Ray Collins, Pallion, Sunderland.

Walkers on the Pennine Way. 'When they finally see the inn, they break into a trot'.

SOME PEOPLE LIKED IᛏT HERE

22. 8.89 This is my second visit to this oasis of ecstasy (almost as good as sex!!).   *Gary Hutton.*

14. 8.89 Brill, Fab. HEAVEN, PARADISE!
                        Nick Williams, Yeovil, 'Zummerset'.

9. 8.89 Today has seen the highest waterfall, the highest rainfall and the highest pub. The last is definitely the best.   *Alastair Paterson, Leicester.*

10. 8.89 After hours of toil along an arduous path . . . what a sight! The best double glazing I've ever seen — but people keep dropping feathers around me while I'm trying to drink my nice cool pint.   *Tim Grix.*

4. 5.89 Enchanting!   *Bill & Jane Lamb, Harrogate.*

5. 5.89 BEAUT VIEWS.   *John Parsons, W. Australia.*

10. 6.89 Nearest we'll ever get to heaven!!!
                        James & Betty Reid, South Humberside.

3. 4.90 God save the Queen & Tan Hill pub.
                        C. E. Longway, Dallas Texas.

WAINWRIGHT

(Author of the standard guide to the Pennine Way)

27. 8.90 Only 146 miles to go. Oh, God, I hate Wainwright.

Mike Thorrell, Leeds.

5. 9.89 Please will people stop talking about Wainwright as if he is God — he is very sexist and racist (read his books), elitist (hates other walkers) and has caused great erosion problems with his out-of-date guide-books.

Pete, Birkenhead.

7. 9.89 When all this is over, I'll send my socks to Mr Wainwright.

Andy Mayo, Leicester.

25. 8.89 Must be bloody daft. Don't use OS maps or Wainwright!

(unsigned).

8. 8.89 'What would I like to do most at the moment?' It is not: to drink a pint of foaming, cool beer: to eat a huge plateful of steak and chips: to fall into the arms of a beautiful girl. No. It's to take hold of Wainwright and to kick him as hard as possible in the balls.

(Signed: Pissed Off, Baslow, Derbyshire.)

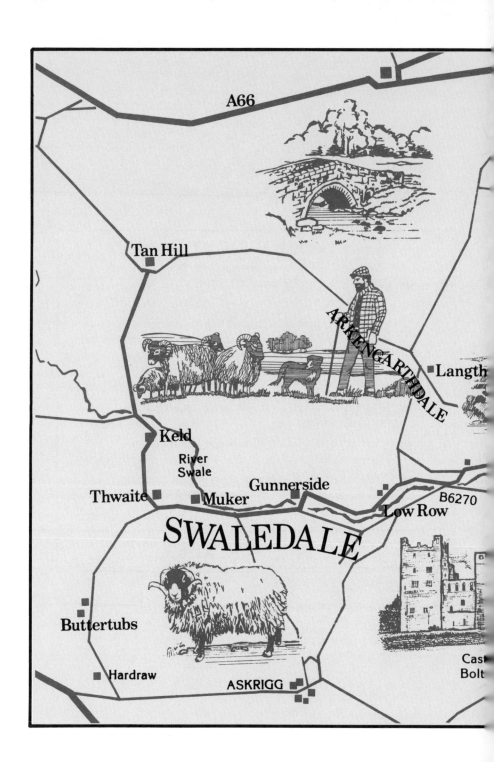

A66

Tan Hill

ARKENGARTHDALE

Langth

Keld

River
Swale

Gunnerside

Thwaite

Muker

Low Row

B6270

SWALEDALE

Buttertubs

Hardraw

ASKRIGG

Cas
Bolt

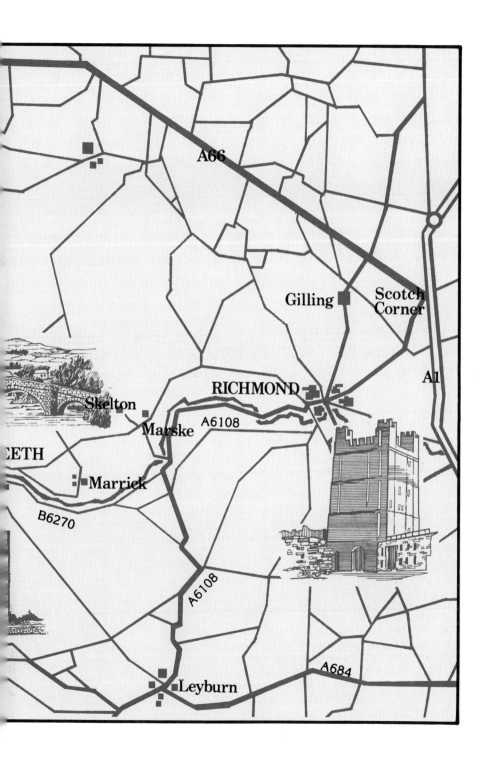

CHAPTER SIX

"WE ONLY COME TO TORMENT THE LANDLORD"

The inn was empty. A feeble January sun drifting through the windows cast a grey light on the stone-flagged floor, still damp from its early-morning scouring. At this dour time of the year, Tan Hill expects little in the way of passing trade.

And with the nearest house about four miles away, there won't be many 'locals' dropping in either. How many of the dalespeople, I asked Margaret, could she count on as regular patrons?

'Five'.

'Not every day, of course. Fridays usually. One of them told the television people. "The landlord says·there's no local trade but we still go there just to torment him".'

'Nobody comes in and sits at the bar every night. If we relied on local trade we'd have given up four years ago.' (The Baines moved in just five years earlier).

The assistant barman chipped in: 'Tan Hill's not like them downtown joints.' "Downtown" in this context meant the pubs in Reeth, or even Richmond, victims of cheerless 'modernisation'.

One of the five 'regulars' at Tan Hill is Clifford Harker. He has lived in Swaledale all his life, a sheep-farmer like his father who introduced him to the inn on the hill at an early age.

'The first time I came here I was only a little kid like and came with my dad on the back of his pushbike. Any time we passed by, we could call in and get a drink. Many times we came in we hadn't the money on us but we could get a drink and pay the next time we came in, see?'

In those days, beer was about 1½d (½p) a pint. It was stored in barrels a few steps down from the single bar-room. 'It'd be a cold place then, up against the outside wall. They'd just have barrels, they'd roll them in in summertime, but in winter they'd never have any gas-beer 'cos the pipes would freeze up. Just bottled beer in winter.'

Bill Calvert also paid his first visit to Tan Hill with his father, driving sheep down the dale. 'My father always had a bottle of milk in his pocket every time he came past Tan Hill. 'Cos all they had up here was a goat and the bugger at that time of year'd by dry, wouldn't it? So he'd fetch them a bottle of milk.

Left — An old engraving of the parlour, date unknown. The fireplace hasn't changed much and even some of the furniture looks suspiciously familiar.

Hand a bottle of milk in the door and we'd have half of beer apiece. I was only a lad and father said "Could I sup a half of beer?" and I said "Well, try me." Aye, two halves of beer out of bottles. It'd be Birtwhistles ale, brewed in Appleby'.

Nowadays, the regulars tend to congregate at Tan Hill on a Friday night. The week's gossip is brought up to date, national and international problems forthrightly disposed of and local concerns aired with a great deal of plain speaking and good humour.

There's little patience with government of any kind: 'They should get off their fat arses, try running a farm, they'd learn summat about earning some daily bread.'

The National Park authorities whose writ runs through Swaledale also come in for a lot of stick.

'They order us. Build your house this way. Use these kind of roof-tiles. Are you sure your windows don't go against some European idea of windows? Everyone in Europe has to have the same kind of window? Can you believe that?'

Most people in the bar did believe it. It was a good debating point: Swaledale people seem to enjoy confronting anyone who tries to tell them what they should be doing. Their instinctive reaction is to do exactly what they intended in the first place, and the National Park bureaucrats can make what they want of it.

Drinkers at the oasis in a wilderness.

Clifford Harker recalls the old days when Sunday night was the time for dalespeople to make their way to Tan Hill. 'We used to come every Sunday night. Just two or three from down Arkengarthdale, two or three from Swaledale. It was always a gathering-place. Jolly nice.'

They were quiet, comforting evenings. In the company of friendly neighbours, you could set the world to rights. And, sitting high above England at Tan Hill, you could take a lofty view of its troubles: few of these local difficulties would survive a healthy draught of local ale.

CHAPTER SEVEN

ONLY HERE FOR THE BEER

For most of its long history, Tan Hill Inn and good beer have been distant strangers.

In mediaeval times, the inn's impoverished patrons paid a groat or so for a wooden, or pewter pot of 'small beer'. This was a watery concoction with an alcohol content — on a good day — of about 2%. Most standard beers on sale nowadays are at least four times as strong.

'Small beer' did have some advantages though. At that strength, you could start the day swallowing a pint with breakfast, slake your thirst with it through the day and still sink a few pints in the evening.

It was also quite nutritious and, perhaps most important, the alcohol made it generally safe to drink. Water supplies at that time were desperately vulnerable to pollution of every kind from seeping sewage to a drowned sheep upstream.

The arrival of bottled beer increased both its strength and its price. Most Tan Hill patrons would still have settled for the murky tap-beer, waiting to give their order perhaps until they saw the landlord about to broach a fresh barrel.

Matters improved dramatically in 1984 when Neil Hanson took over as landlord. Together with Theakstons, a long established Yorkshire brewery, he launched a campaign to improve the quality of pub beer, not just at Tan Hill but throughout the country.

His *'Good Beer Guide'* to the best hostelries in England proved so successful he abandoned the inn for a full-time career as a writer.

Theakstons stayed on. After all, the Theakston family had been in Yorkshire a very long time, arriving with the hooligan Viking hordes who terrorised northern Britain in the 8th century.

A thousand years later, the Theakstons had settled down a bit. In 1827, Robert Theakston, from his Black Bull brewhouse in Masham, began acquiring inns throughout North Yorkshire and supplying their cellars with his strong-flavoured, long-tasting beers.

In an inspired public relations move, Robert appropriated one of the best logos of any British brewery — the Seal of the Official of the Peculier of Masham.

The seal shows in its centre a man in Arab dress kneeling in front of two mosques. The usual explanation is very complicated, involving ransoms for captured Crusaders and an Archbishop of York who couldn't be bothered with administering Masham church.

Right — Alec and Margaret Baines celebrate a Tan Hill rarity
— a warm Summer's day.

Instead, he granted them a 'peculier' court of their own. In the Norman-French language of the time, the 'peculier of Masham' simply meant the court was 'special to' the town.

It was invested with extensive powers. Amongst other things, it could fine or even imprison you for:
- Not coming to church enough
- Keeping a hat on at communion time
- Bidding the churchwardens to do their worst when they asked your to go to church
- Telling fortunes or using enchantments
- Harbouring Roman Catholic priests
  and, (revealing a highly improbable cure for insomnia)
- Carrying a dead man's skull out of the churchyard and laying it under the head of a person to charm him to sleep.

A few pints of 'Old Peculier' would have had the same effect with much more comfort.

CHAPTER EIGHT

"ANYONE WHO LIVES AT TAN HILL ALL YEAR IS PRETTY BRAVE"

Tan Hill Inn sits in the middle of a wasteland. All the services most of us take for granted: water, electricity, sewerage, telephones, stop short by many miles of this isolated house.

So, you use a radio-telephone, you install diesel-powered generators for lighting and heat, and you make sure there's enough coal lodged in the bunkers to see you through the winter.

There still remains the problem of getting enough water. When the Baines arrived, the only water that reached the pub came from an arthritic 'ram' pump a quarter of a mile away that sucked at a mountain stream and struggled to deliver it to the inn. In winter it froze, in summer it was gasping for water. For the rest of the year, it worked quite well.

Then a water-diviner visited the inn. He was quite sure that unlimited quantities of water were lying beneath Tan Hill: how far down he didn't know. His twigs would tell him.

Alec was convinced, and the dowser patrolled up and down, arms outstretched, his hazel twig jerking into life every so often. At last, with an agitated twitching, it indicated the right place to bore.

For more than a week, workmen drilled their way into the earth. At a depth of 168 feet water suddenly spouted up the tubes: from now on, Tan Hill had its own water supply. Cost: £3,000.

So there was no longer any need for the old septic toilet which had to be emptied by staff wearing rubber gloves. It used to be an outside privy, a shed perched on the hillside a few yards from the house. 'Nothing wrong with it' said one regular visitor, 'the wind dried it out, took the smell away'.

Old photographs of the inn show another house just to the west, now demolished. A coal-miner used to live there. When he retired he went to live down the dale but got fed up and returned. 'It was too quiet for him down there'. Despite its remoteness, Tan Hill is never dull.

When the Baines arrived, they worried at first that their three children would feel isolated. 'But I think they basically enjoy it up here,' says Margaret. 'They meet an awful lot of people. Better off here than they are in a town: no worries about where they are at night.'

Kim, the youngest, goes to the primary school in Langthwaite, nine miles away: Kirsty has a twenty-two-mile journey to her school in Richmond. 'We go five miles down the road and meet a bus. One goes at 7.30, the other at 8.15 so we make two trips. We do forty miles a day just getting 'em to bus, two hours a day just going up and down. It's very time-consuming, especially in summer when we're busy.'

Left — Loading up at Tan Hill mine.
There was no weighing-machine — a few pounds either way bothered no-one.

(And, in winter, it's a different problem. For six weeks during their first winter here, snow-blocked roads stopped the children getting to school at all.)

Making sure that the larder is well-stocked also requires careful planning. 'A shop in Reeth used to deliver but they've closed now. So I take the pick-up to Penrith - about forty miles away - to the Cash and Carry'.

Then there's the difficulty of finding staff prepared to share their secluded house. 'You have to get on together. If they can't drive, they can't go anywhere. We do have a little van for them to run out in. But everybody lives on top of each other — you've no time for yourself. If you want a night off, you can't stay in the pub. There's always someone wants to see you'.

Despite all the problems, the Baines feel a responsibility to provide hospitality at all times for any chance wayfarer. 'We do try to stay open. We might get only two or three people a day, but they've come to see us, or the pub anyway, and the nearest one is miles away. So you do feel you have to have everything ready.'

Right — An early view of Tan Hill that became a popular postcard.

Tan Hill Inn.

11 miles from Kirkby Stephen. Highest Public House in England. 1732 ft.

'Every day', says Margaret, 'I'll write the menu out on the blackboard, but sometimes you do feel it's a waste of time.' Though much appreciated. Margaret fondly recalls the American visitor who asked her for the recipe for a Yorkshire pudding she had taken from the freezer a few minutes earlier.

The rigours of life at Tan Hill entail some compromises. 'It's a totally different world here. You go to other pubs and you see landladies with all their jewellery on, it just wouldn't go here. If I go into the bar in a skirt, everybody's saying, "What's up?", "Where are you going"?'

At present, the Baines have no thoughts of going anywhere else. Within the space of a few years, they have revitalised a pub that had been sliding into decay. They have endured two of the most savage winters the dale has known for many years, skillfully established Tan Hill as a tourist attraction and, by building a 14-bed extension, restored its reputation as a genuine inn.

Perhaps the most telling testimony to the Baines' determination came from a local farmer seated at the bar one evening. His land lay a little further down the dale: his battles with terrain and climate only a mite less implacable.

But his respect for the Baines was evident: "Anyone who lives at Tan Hill all year round is pretty brave, to say the least."

CHAPTER NINE

"IT'S THE ROYAL SHOW FOR SWALEDALE SHEEP IS TAN HILL FAIR"

Spring comes very late in Swaledale: at Tan Hill it often seems reluctant to arrive at all.

It's not unusual for the surrounding moors to be covered by several feet of snow well into May.

But however foul the weather may be, the Swaledale Sheep Fair will always go ahead on the last Thursday in May.

The normally deserted road leading to Tan Hill is suddenly swamped by cattle-vans. Ranks of bewildered sheep find themselves ushered into pens where their windswept fleeces are groomed with as much attention as in a London hair salon.

'It's the Royal Show for Swaledale sheep is Tan Hill Fair' said one farmer. 'There are classes for Swaledale sheep at the Royal but there are sheep that can win at the Royal might not get a ticket here. Far superior what you get here than what it is at the big shows.'

It's not the prizes though which attract exhibitors from all across the north of England — the top award at Tan Hill won't even cover your travelling expenses.

But the prestige of winning at Tan Hill is something else. A recent prize-winner won a few pounds as best in its class. A few days later it went to auction in Hawes: the Tupp Hogg went off to stud, its former owner returned home richer by £30,000.

At one of the first Swaledale Sheep fairs, John Thompson displays his prize tup.

Sheep dominate life in Swaledale. They're a major part of its economy, their welfare an abiding subject of conversation wherever two or three farmers are gathered together.

Even the most casual visitor to the dale can't miss them. On remote hillsides, they fix walkers with a penetrating glare: on the busiest roads, they treat summer traffic with a leisurely disdain.

With their black faces, grey noses and curled horns, they look remarkably intelligent. They were certainly sensible enough to grow two separate coats of wool to cope with the ferocious Swaledale winters.

An outer covering of rugged wool shrugs off the assaults of rain, sleet and snow. Beneath that, an even tougher coat preserves the animal's body heat. Swaledale wool is highly prized by climbers and mountaineers for its resistance to cold and damp but, by the early 1970's, the old skills of knitting this wiry fibre had almost died out.

Then a group of local people led by the vicar of Muker, a few miles down the dale, looked for ways of reviving the traditional craft.

The Keld Brass Band often played for festive events at Tan Hill.

Groomed for stardom, three Swaledale Sheep go off to the fair.

It wasn't the first time the industry had been in trouble. In 1571, for example, Elizabeth I had tried to stimulate demand by decreeing that her subjects should wear knitted woollen caps on Sundays and holidays).

Four hundred years later, the Muker rescue attempt has been highly successful. An old stone cottage in the village serves as a showcase for Swaledale Woollens where the sweaters, gloves and cardigans on sale carry labels bearing the names of the knitters who created them. Many of these names are the same as those appearing in the old hand-knitters registers of the 16th century.

Tan Hill fair is now such an established part of Swaledale life it's surprising to discover that it only began in 1951. There had been earlier fairs, of course — the one at Thwaite was particularly popular. But by the mid-1930s, they had all fallen victim to depopulation and the Depression.

Much of the credit for reviving a Swaledale fair belongs to local farmers like Clifford Harker. His clean-cut features chiselled by moorland winds, he is, understandably, an enthusiastic promoter of Swaledale sheep.

The prizes are small but there is enormous prestige in winning at Tan Hill.

'People think they all look alike, but they're all different, characters you could say.' The original decision to hold the fair in late May respected the natural rhythm of life in dale.

'It's just spring o't'year — you've just got finished lambing, you see, it's the first time you can get away.

A day out, like. And it's in everybody's mind — the Swaledale show. We needn't really advertise but we do do. Everyone really knows it's that day, last Thursday in May. We have a fair like, but it's not the usual kind of show, fair attractions and such, nothing like that — just sheep.

If you've no interest in sheep, you don't come to Tan Hill fair. There's one or two stands — sheep dip, Barbour coats, wellingtons and such and that's it.

But it's a picture to see. Look one way or t'other, sheep, sheep. I don't know if general stock's improved but t'shape of champions has. A lot of money put in there, tha' knows that. And without a good pub like this, the show couldn't be safe.'

In the kitchen, Margaret is busy. Large plates are heaped high with meat, vegetables and succulent Yorkshire puddings. Not everyone can leave the fair with a rosette: they can all leave with a well-lined stomach.

CHAPTER TEN

'COUNTIES IN BRAWL OVER HIGHEST PUB'

(NEWSPAPER HEADLINE, SEPTEMBER 1988)

For centuries, no-one had any doubt that Tan Hill Inn was a Yorkshire pub. True, it stood perilously close to the border with County Durham: maybe part of the back rooms straddled the county line. But most visitors to Tan Hill felt confident they were supping Yorkshire ale in a Yorkshire Inn.

The bureaucrats who master-minded the Local Government Act of 1974 took a different view. Seen from Whitehall, the tiny speck on the Ordnance Survey maps that represented Tan Hill Inn could quite conveniently be drafted into Durham.

A tidy solution, but one that didn't satisfy the patrons of Tan Hill. Or the Baines. They joined the struggle to return Tan Hill to Yorkshire.

Speaking to a local newspaper, Margaret declared 'As far as I'm concerned, it's a bit silly us being in Durham. The dustbins are emptied by Richmond council, the road is cleared by North Yorkshire, my children go to school in Yorkshire. And we also sell Yorkshire beer. The only real connection with Durham is we are policed from there — and that means a 40-mile round trip for them from Barnard Castle.'

'We've always considered the pub to be in Yorkshire,' Alec added. 'And we've stuck to the Yorkshire address.'

County Durham based its claim to Tan Hill on the fact that the narrow road running just south of the pub, (in official parlance it's known as the C29A road) clearly places the inn just north of it and so within their territory.

In the end, it wasn't local sentiment or historic claims that decided which county Tan Hill belonged to. It was the accountants at Durham County Council who decided that Tan Hill was too expensive for them. Getting the Baines' children to school cost £7,600 a year in fares, keeping open the roads to the inn, about £8,000.

Their Chief Executive, Peter Dawson, told a special meeting of the County Council's Policy and Resources committee: 'The fact is, we don't have a powerful case against the boundary change on the technical front and even if we did we would be taking on a financial liability.'

Durham County Council members didn't take long to decide that any financial liability really belonged to Yorkshire. There followed many months during which the Whitehall mandarins agonized over the small print of ancient documents. Their long-considered decision in favour of returning Tan Hill to Yorkshire surprised no-one but themselves: where else but in Yorkshire could Tan Hill find a home?

Right — The owner of a Tan Hill coalmine poses with some of his workers.

When the officials confirmed what everyone knew, Alec met the press. 'We're really pleased at the news,' he said. 'Let's hope they leave us alone now.' But they didn't. Teesdale District Council objected to losing the inn (and its rateable value) and its drawing-power for visitors to the area.

They were too late. On April 1st, 1991, Tan Hill inn was officially restored to the county most visitors regard as its natural home: Yorkshire.

But the bureaucrats never give up. An extract from Margaret's diary for December 6th, 1990: 'Battle with Teesdale council over Euroslates for the roof which to 99½% of the population look identical if not better than stone. They agreed to them two years and now they've changed their minds.

We've also been told to take the porch down, which admittedly was built without permission but is a necessity at Tan Hill.'

CHAPTER ELEVEN

"OUR WINTERS ARE SOMETHING SPECIAL"

When the Baines arrived at Tan Hill, Margaret decided to keep a diary recording their most dramatic moments.

It wasn't long before she found herself covering the pages.

'You wouldn't believe the pub could be flooded. The highest pub in England. But it was. Water was coming through the back door like a river. The toilets were a good six inches under water and you needed wellies to play in the pool room.'

It was all the fault of Hurricane Charlie which dumped four inches of rain on the Pennines in twelve hours — the normal rainfall for a month.

'At least we were better off than the people down the dale. The water did run away from us.'

At Low Row, Mr Frank Rodber of Richmond was forced to cling to the top of a telephone box as the torrent swept around his car. Fortunately, before climbing onto the roof he managed to make a 999 call.

Mrs Avril Richardson, the post-mistress at Langthwaite, described how the floodwaters had ripped through the picturesque village in the early hours. 'It came down very quickly like a wall of water. Greenhouses, sheds and all sorts were just washed away . . . I've never seen anything like it.'

A retired miner, Mr John Goodall, was asleep in his caravan at Reeth when the deluge struck. 'I woke up to find my caravan moving. I looked outside and there was three feet of water flowing past.'

Near the hamlet of Whaw, a family of four — and their dog — was plucked to safety by an RAF Sea King helicopter. The rainstorm was the worst on record since the great tempest of 1899 which virtually destroyed the village of Thwaite. Its riverside gardens were engulfed and it was said that flowers planted at Thwaite bloomed the next year at Muker, two miles downstream.

Such rains are unusual: the persistent Pennine winds are not. 'Most days you can't put any washing on the line, it'd be scattered from here to Scotland.' And Margaret still recalls with awe the day when the postman was delivered by the wind. 'He weighed about 15 stone, but when he stepped out of his van, the wind just picked him up and dropped him at the door.'

'Wind? They should have a notice in these parts, "Beware of low-flying sheep!"'

Fog? 'Here you can't see across the road. You just go ten minutes down the road and it's clear as a bell.'

In the bar, the weather is a constant subject of conversation: how bad it was yesterday, how foul it is today and how much worse it will be tomorrow. 'If it rains then turns to snoaw, then that is the worst.'

'It's always a white Christmas at Tan Hill' says Margaret. 'You hear the weather forecasts, Oh, there's no snow in England and we're sitting here with snow half-way up the windows. Unless you've actually lived here, you wouldn't believe what could happen in a matter of hours.'

Right — Tan Hill Inn during the winter of 1936.

On such days, you can watch an interesting ritual dance in front of the bar-room fire. One after another, the farmers plant their backsides to the heat, step away and pause before sitting down again. The pause is important: if you sit down too quickly you may find yourself with third-degree burns on your buttocks.

During the Baines' first winter here they were cut off for six weeks. 'There was ice four inches thick inside the windows. The beer froze in the pipes, the spirit bottles shattered. We had to melt snow for drinking water.'

'The lemonade all froze in t'bottles. When you went in beer cellar, it were quite funny 'cos lemonade swells up when it freezes, there was just this broken glass around the lemonade. Someone did suggest trying to save it but I thought powdered glass in lemonade could have been a bad idea.'

The next three winters were unusually clement: Margaret's diary shows few entries until December 8th, 1990.

'I came down to make the tea, opened the door to let the dog out and was met by a solid wall of snow. The whole pub at the front is an igloo. We can't open doors or windows — not that we're going anywhere or can see anything for the blizzard outside.

Billy (one of the barmen) came back from feeding the hens with a bucket-full of frozen bodies which we thawed out in front of the fire so now the bar's full of grateful hens. We haven't found the twenty ducks yet. So here we are stuck in the highest pub in England with no electric, no water, no customers and no roof but as much snow inside as outside. One thing Billy did say, he would let us have what water was left and he would tolerate drinking beer.'

Right — The ever-burning fire at Tan Hill provides warmth for a rescued lamb.

December 9th: 'The kids have a great snowslide from the bedroom window on to what was the Land Rover and into a drift. They're cold but happy. Things must be bad though — we've just watched The Waltons on television.'

In the kitchen, snow blowing in through the air vent over the gas stove had piled on the hood, melted and dowsed the burners. Turning the invader against itself, Alec blocked every possible entrance to the house with a wad of hand-crushed snow.

Despite the atrocious weather, there were still visitors. 'Six Pennine Way walkers came in, desperate for a beer. They stood there in a row holding the beer-line in their hands to thaw it out so they could have a pint.'

Perhaps the most typical entry in Margaret's diary is for Spring Bank Holiday Monday, 1986:

'The weather is excellent. No snow for two whole days. In true Tan Hill style we carry on in vain. The TV stopped working on Thursday, the generator packed up on Sunday afternoon and now we've just said goodbye to the microwave.'

FIRST – AND LAST – IMPRESSIONS

Edmund Bogg in 1909: 'Tan Hill stands, apart from a whitewashed gable porch, plain, gaunt, grey and unlovely externally, on the road line of the water-parting between the Tees and the Swale.'

Landlord Neil Hanson in 1984: 'A gaunt stone building covered in cracked and collapsing rendering, painted a hideous mustard-yellow.'

The Swaledale historian Ella Pontefract in the 1920s: 'It is solitary on most days, the only sign of life a goat silhouetted against the white wall of the porch.' She found the interior much more inviting, noting the old kitchen with its scoured stone floor, the gleaming brasses hung around the fireplace and a bright list rug before the fire.

Most visitors remarked on the ever-burning fire, a suitable symbol for the inn since 'tan' is the old Celtic word for fire. On May Day, the Celts kindled 'beltane' fires on the hills: 'Baal fires' in worship of Baal and the sun. (At Tan Heol in Brittany the custom lasted well into the twentieth century).

The goat at Tan Hill was another important feature. Newly wedded couples were encouraged to stop off at the inn to drink the goat milk, after which they would be blessed with many children.

But the special character of Tan Hill is found in its people. Dalesmen like Dick who made just one journey out of the district to visit the Smithfield show. Arriving at King's Cross he took one look at the grubby buildings, the hurrying crowds and caught the next train back.

One tourist stopped off for a pint, then stayed for four days sleeping in a tent pitched on the moor. Running out of money, he returned to London for more cash, re-appearing at Tan Hill to stay for several weeks.

According to Hilaire Belloc, "An inn is of the nation that made it . . . inns are the mirror and at the same time the flower of a people."

In less high-flown language, anyone who visits the ancient inn on Tan Hill steps into a very special environment where the traditional virtues of the English pub survive in robust good health.

ACKNOWLEDGEMENTS

The author's warmest thanks are due to Alec and Margaret Baines and their family for their hospitality and their unfailing patience in responding to his endless questions.

Thanks are also due to David Joy, editor of THE DALESMAN and the North of England Open Air Museum, Beamish, for permission to reproduce the photographs on pages 16, 17, 19, 41, 54, 68, and 76.

The original painting of Tan Hill on the cover is by Ashley Jackson.

Finally, thanks to Duncan Allison whose idea it was to produce this tribute to one of England's most interesting inns.